Lapsed Capit
A Poetry Colle

ISBN: 9781916320086
Imprint: Independently published

The Poems

Lapsed Capitalist

I was raised as a Capitalist
Baptized within days
Into this religion
And taught of its ways

Anointed with gifts
And shiny new toys
Dressed in the new clothes
To fit in with the boys

Enrolled in a school
Sure of my success
Examined and measured
To earn more than less

All too soon was ordained
And began my career
Sacrificing my dreams
On the altar of fear

Confessed of my sins
When I took a day's rest
To pause from the grind
Or to feel at my best

Lapsed Capitalist cont.

Married a Capitalist
Was soon with a child
Began to imagine
How their life would be styled

Reflected upon
My religion of old
Should I pass to my child
The faith I had been sold?

Would I want this for him?
Should he make his own mind?
Was it fair to impose?
Would he leave it behind?

I was raised as a Capitalist
Now my faith's all but gone
But I still hear its gospel
In the prayers of my son

I Saved a Life Today

I saved a life today
Rescued from burning bridge
Pulled back from bridge ledge

Laid rugs on stony ground
Poured tea into empty cups
Rubbed balm into dry hands

Filled belly with hot soup
Chatted into silent ears
Wiped tears from damp eyes

Made smile sunken mouth
Made light heavy heart
Made strong weakened spirit

I saved a life today

Seaside Hotel

They're making cards in the craft room
For a Christmas I won't see
For this pain in my bones
It will be the death of me

When I eat my stomach tells me
It can no longer digest
Though the waitress who observes me
Says I only speak in jest

And bell boys run down corridors
On hearing shrill alarms
Find guests requests for room service
Another order for self harm

While visits to the concierge
In my slipper and my socks
Sees me ask for just some fresh air
And I key to turn the locks

But these dreams are just a memory
I checked out to touch the sea
Though I still think of my fellow guests
Less fortunate than me

Castle

I will build a castle inside of me
I will build it strong and fine
It will house the heart and soul of me
This mighty home of mine

I will set foundations deep within
And turrets towards the sky
Windows looking out on mountains
And the people who pass by

I will set a drawbridge in the walls
To go out and come back in
And only welcome those who'll love
The rooms beneath my skin

How We Tell Our Story Matters

How we tell our story matters
How to others and within
Whether shouting or through whispers
We are always listening

Where we stand affects our sight line
How we see edges and curves
Where we press our hearts upon it
Sensing what we should deserve

Sometimes holding it above us
Where it casts a shadow wide
Blocking out the power of sunlight
Gives a common place to hide

Sometimes standing firm upon it
Feel it moulded to our feet
Never letting us move freely
Just to make us feel complete

Sometimes distancing us from it
Running fast to keep it far
But when asked to tell our story
Question who we really are

We can hold its hand while walking
Like a friend who knows us well
With the knowledge of the magic
In the words we choose to tell

We can listen but forgive it
Give a kinder point of view
As we would with such a good friend
So they might see things anew

How We Tell Our Story Matters con.

How we tell our story matters
How to others and within
Whether shouting or through whispers
We are always listening
We are always listening
We are always listening
We are always listening

Long Sleep in Springtime

Yesterday afternoon
It was Spring
I was walking by the river
Sun touching my face

Last night I had the strangest dream
Everything we once took for granted
We could no longer do
And with such dreams as these
I kept trying to wake up

We listened every day to the news
For signs of hope and a return
To things we could no longer do
And with such dreams as these
I kept trying to wake up

But this morning
It was Spring again
I took a walk by the river
And felt the sun touching my face

The Poor Are Not to be Trusted

The poor are not to be trusted with money
They won't make deals in offshore accounts
They'll just keep towns alive and thriving
By exchanges of their small amounts

The poor will only choose to spend it
They won't invest in stocks and shares
They're known for making bad decisions
Being ignorant of economic affairs

The poor don't know to feed their children
They'll spend on things they shouldn't need
That's why they must be always denied it
And kept by those who favour greed

No the poor are not to be trusted with money
We shouldn't provide or should we lend
It must be pushed through several channels
Beginning with our donor friends

New Curriculum

We're replacing History with
How Did We Get Here?
Geography with
Respect for the Earth
Economics with
How Money is Stolen
And RE
What's a Human Worth?
We're replacing Politics with
The Stories We're Moved By
Languages with
Being a Friend
Literature with
Understanding Our Own Selves
And Technology
How to Repair and Mend
We're Replacing Science with
How We're Connected
Art with
Seeing Things Through Fresh Eyes
Sport with
Excelling Through Teamwork
And Education with
How to Stay Wise

Refuge

I remember your house as a refuge
Away from the worries and cares
Sat in your lounge or your kitchen
Just talking in separate chairs
Or closing our eyes for a moment
Where we found a brief break in the day
Amidst all the books and the paintings
Where we kept the bad dreams far away
I remember that day in your study
When you found me there sat without light
And I thought 'If I could stay here'
Where there'd be no more reasons to fight
I remember a place I found safety
In the rooms an oasis of calm
When the noise of the past turned to silence
And there seemed no place further from harm
I remember when I felt in danger
And I ran to your house from the flood
But your house wasn't where I'd remembered
In its place just some rubble and mud
Had a bomb just been thrown through a window?
Leaving dust where there once had been bricks
Now I wonder was that house a real house
As I do know the mind can play tricks

More Birds in the Markets than Forests

More birds in the markets than forests
The male birds are losing their song
They can't learn from fathers and brothers
Their tunes to know where they belong

The females can't hear from their species
The males sing a worrying call
So stay far away from each other
Their voice growing ever more small

And that means they can't get together
To mate and make more songbirds sing
So music from birds grows more silent
And that is a terrible thing

Because of the human obsession
To take and not leave things to be
Treats nature to be bought and traded
And our Earth a commodity

The sounds of the forest alert us
Towards the whole health of our Earth
A silent Earth will never nourish
Our children not yet given birth

The Ending of an Era

In the salons of Vienna
Ending of the First World War
Discussing all the artists
And what their muses saw

Defeated by a virus
That spread throughout mankind
So many of its victims
Still young with hope to find

Took Klimt and Egon Schiele
Who shook society
Whose pictures were described by some
As vile monstrosities

Imagining the female form
In ways they's never seen
With eyes and lips expressing
The mind behind the sheen

The ending of an era
A new one just begun
The artists gave a glimpse into
The age which was to come

We Are Suspended

In a moment
We are suspended
Between an old life
Which is dying
And a new life
Which promises refreshment

In a day
We are suspended
Between an old life
Which is dying
And a new life
Which promises renewal

In a night
We are suspended
Between an old life
Which is dying
And a new life
Which promises rejuvenation

In a year
We are suspended
Between an old life
Which is dying
And a new life
Which promises reconnection

Stage Door

Have I relied on my old lines?
Playing parts that I think others seek
Happy to be in the spotlight
Hiding all that I fear could be weak?

There's a stage door that's just within arm's reach
Though it seems to be part of the wall
But when looking through frightened and tired eyes
It appears to be not there at all

Have I ever kept my profile hidden?
As an actor who might wear a mask
Sick with worry and nerves for a question
So relieved when it never gets asked?

There's a stage door that's just within arm's reach
But how long it stays hidden from view
If my thoughts block all knowledge of exits
And an option to see things anew

Have I ever felt folded as paper?
Like an old script tossed down on a stage
Forgetting the patterns within me
Can leak through the lines on a page?

There's a stage door that's just within arm's reach
And the footlights are guiding my feet
I can now see the door in its outline
Where I'll find a new life on the street

With Regret

With regret we have very bad news
From today you are no longer you
All the things that once made you yourself
Now removed so you'll have to get through

From tomorrow we'll wait by the aisles
As an audience sits in the stalls
On a balcony above a lit stage
To anticipate how you'll enthral

From today you should change who you are
Forget all things that once fulfilled
All those years that you'd worked so hard for
And the discipline habits instilled

From tomorrow we'll hear you prepare
As an orchestra tunes up to play
Where a curtain waits long to be raised
On the costumes you once put away

From today put your old self to rest
Find a draw or perhaps an old case
Hope you won't disappear in the dark
While a new you is found to replace

From tomorrow we hope you return
Find those dark parts we asked you to pause
Take them into the spotlight again
Where you'll stand for our stored up applause

The Year of the Quiet Ocean

The year of the quiet ocean
Forced a sudden abrupt hush
With a slowness in the water
Little need for us to rush

When the volume of our world
Was reduced enough to hear
Sounds of nature's reemergence
Though it always had been near

Sound is light to our marine life
Lets them see under the blue
So the silence of our engines
Gives us both a clearer view

Human decibels turned lower
Make way for a symphony
Can we go a little slower
For our friends under the sea?

The Seven Principles of Public Life

The seven principles of public life
Values for those who serve
Selflessness and Integrity
No less than we deserve
Objectivity and Accountability
Values for those who serve
Openness and Honesty
No less than we deserve
Leadership of public leaders
Values for those who serve
A privilege in public life
No less than we deserve

Where Shall We Meet?

Where we give our full attention
With our generosity
Where we'll treat each as an equal
Using curiosity

Where we'll notice how our viewpoints
Might prevent us seeing clear
Knowing how our own prejudgements
Might replace our love with fear

Where we'll hear only to listen
Seeing with each other's eyes
Giving thought to what we're hearing
Leaving out prepared replies

Where our reconciliation
Comes before one's sides defeat
Where connection is the victor
That's a good place we can meet

After the Abolition of Slavery

How to talk about our country?
Deepened fault lines scar the land
Where the path divides before birth
Asks us now to understand

Slavery at last abolished
But what next for those back then?
Owners given compensation
Saw their power begin again

Institutions built on profits
Of the dark Atlantic trade
Now their buildings in our cities
Tell us how their debts were paid

Statues

I want to visit statues
To know why they were made
These statues tell the stories
We pass down and relay

Those lives behind the statues
How did they earn their praise?
And would we honour if we
Knew what we know today?

I know threads must connect me
To names upon the plaques
How do these threads affect me?
I want to know the facts

How did they earn their marble?
When will they be replaced?
How long must they be polished?
And why are they defaced?

They tell me of the people
The statue's figures knew
What stories might they tell me?
I want to know the truth

In Loneliness In Solitude.

In loneliness how I was lost
Within a crowded place
Until I fled to find a room
A solitary space

In solitude how I was found
Heard whispers in my soul
But in my still and quiet spot
Began to hear its gold

In loneliness how I was lost
To fade more every day
Until I almost disappeared
With nothing left to say

In solitude how I was met
With such a fragile hand
Who spoke another language which
I learned to understand

In loneliness how I was feared
Absorbing all I saw
Consuming all the cruellest words
As blows to bruise my core

In solitude how I was loved
And so I built my gate
Without the words I won't endure
Within my happy state

Let Me State the Facts

You're looking at the data wrong
So let me state the facts
I'll tell you what you should have known
It's not true we were lax

The evidence we had back then
Is different from today
Had we the foresight I believe
We'd do the same I'd say

I've had the training so I can
Plant doubt within your mind
Debates I've won a thousand times
I'm not the losing kind

Regardless of the questions asked
I'll get my message through
And if you leave fully confused
I'll have won over you

The Amateur Anthropologist

The amateur anthropologist
Sits quietly in her seat
Observing cafe society
Now its subjects start to meet

Do that group there know each other?
Or have they only met
But they offer pointed elbows
So they can't be too close yet

And at another table
A tribal elder drinks
While younger members sit apart
Respectfully she thinks

The participant observer
Ends her report and presses 'Send'
After months of lonely coffees
She jumps up to hug her friend

The Magician

Drawing thoughts and painting pictures
Draughts it out on paper filled
Constructs worlds we will inhabit
This magician starts to build

Laying tracks for us to travel
Engineering in our mind
Maps to guide us to locations
This magician starts to find

Makes a bridge to pass obstruction
Leaping over narrow straits
Throwing stepping stones to tread on
This magician will create

Hearing thoughts as plans for certain
What was image soon we'll feel
Weaving spells with words we tell it
This magician makes it real

A Billion

We've offered a billion to children
A billion is sure to impress
Don't ask me how that makes an impact
That's certain to heal their distress

For a billion you're meant to be grateful
Despite more we're spending on war
It's only a child's education
Something you should be thankful for

Your eyes should light up for a billion
Unlike critics you might have read
A humongous amount is a billion
Ignore just how thin that will spread

Thought Leaders

Thought leaders are certain
We must move at pace
Deliver at scale
To win in this race

Move forward on purpose
Intentionally so
Hold on to the vision
And never let go

Engage all the team
To get all on board
Ensure all the comms
Cannot be ignored

Assess the skills base
Identify holes
So no one in here
Denies us our goals

Be more than efficient
To Hell with the stress
And when we're exhausted
We'll toast our success

Rewild

Rewild the concrete office tower
To make a shady leafy bower
Let all the cutters rest today
And watch the meadow grasses sway

Rewild the centre of the roads
Make bridges for the crossing toads
Replant the trees so long cut down
To make a car park for the town

Rewild the roof tops stark and bare
So butterflies might thrive up there
Let neat lawns long resist the mow
Give flowers a simple chance to grow

Rewild the waters leaving free
The creatures living in the sea
Turn off the engines deafening roar
So mammals can be heard once more

Rewild the kitchen with the seeds
That gives us all our body needs
The plants that nourish soothe and heal
Restoring us with every meal

Rewild our minds so we recall
We're not apart from Earth at all
Our every atom every cell
Relies on nature being well

How to Define Corruption

How to define corruption
To aid and to abet
A sorry lack of candour
Something we should regret

How to define a process
Which only tries to block
And statements give no answers
To relatives in shock

How to define transparent
When nothing seems quite clear
As papers are found shredded
And people disappear

How to define concealment
To keep an image clean
Maintain a reputation
Reverse what words can mean

How to define a system
Opaque just as a cloud
Ungraspable confusing
To stir an angry crowd

How to define endemic
Betraying trust long earned
So grateful for inquiries
And lessons to be learned

How to define persistence
For those we can't forget
Long weary but still fighting
Until justice is met

Hidden Texts Kept Unofficial

Hidden texts kept unofficial
Private Email WhatsApp feed
No communication's off bounds
When it comes to our pure greed

Personal accounts kept in secret
Knowing they won't be disclosed
So our sordid machinations
Won't be suddenly exposed

Leave no paper trail behind us
Let the public speculate
We'll convince them with our answers
On the morning news debate

If we say it's all above board
And repeat repeat that phrase
Let's just hope we get away with
Our dark dealings and sly ways

First Lesson At The Boarding School

A sudden break from family
Creates the stoic kind
First lesson at the boarding school
Detach the heart from mind

Next lesson to despise the ones
Who live within the town
Who go home every night unlike
The new friends you have found

Emotional detachment
A cure for missing home
Turns into growing arrogance
Makes one feel less alone

The ones who can go home for tea
Are mocked with made up names
While in this gilded prison you
Can play your sports and games

Ambition just a substitute
To hide the deadened self
A single minded focus leads
To power, fame and wealth

An in that role there'll always be
A need to make a team
Connections from the dormitory
Who'll know just what you mean

Then schooldays can return and
Back playing on the pitches
Still demonising those who did
Not benefit from riches

As Orwell the Etonian
Was changed by what he saw
One hopes you're moved today and then
Compassion is restored

Impeccable Credentials

Impeccable credentials
Connected supremely
Quintessential services
These things will not come free

To clients of a concierge
Wishes come easily
Now access to the party board's
Included in the fee

Donations without influence
The co chairman will see
His clients get their meetings
With number one MP

Business meets with politics
For dates with royalty
Investors don't expect returns
It's purely charity

A cosy little nexus
Ensure's power's not shared
And only those with millions
Can get their voices heard

Remember All the Fun We Had?

Remember all the fun we had at university?
And now I've been appointed to a Standards Committee

To recommend, assess, correct in short to oversee
Completely independent and appointed correctly

My emailed application was considered carefully
I have no formal power it's strictly advisory

But

How can I be objective with connections so friendly?
I even helped you fund raise at a party recently

Who hasn't seen that photo when our club was male only?
It's rumoured you have brought me in recruited desperately

And now my role's to question your decisions ethically
Remembering the fun we had at university

Goodbye 1983

Let's stop discrimination
For the next generation
Let our children not fear
The stigma witnessed here

Let the language we share
Make us aware
Of inside injury
Same as physically

Both with parity
Seen equally
Talk openly
Set each one free

Let's stop discrimination
For the next generation
Let our children not fear
The stigma witnessed here

The Right Path

The right path is always uphill
There's always a new step to make
There's effort in climbing to find the next view
We'll admire when we take a brief break

There's risk in ascending towards a new goal
Only those who stand still never fall
But better to lift ourselves up when we do
Than never to stumble at all

Storytelling Through Seven Stories

In the sea I am lost in the dark night
With a book of blank pages in hand
They await for the lines and the chapters
To explain how I'll find my dry land

Will my oars have to slay a great monster?
After voyage will this boat return?
Will the journey be simply comedic?
Or a quest for a truth I must learn?

Will my rags be transformed into riches?
Will I know a transforming rebirth?
Not one story will end for me tragic
While I'm sailing my boat here on Earth

On Waking Up To The Shipping Forecast

Viking: How Could She?
North Utsire: Why didn't he?
South Utsire: This is unfair
Forties: Who else was there?
Cromerty: I wasn't heard
Forth: This is absurd
Tyne: I've been misled
Dogger: Just what's been said?
Fisher: I'm feeling bruised
German Bight: Once more abused
Humber: I see your light
Thames: Admire your fight
Dover: Stay straight and strong
Wight: You won't go wrong
Portland: You know what's right
Plymouth: I sense the light
Biscay: To love our shade
Trafalgar: How we've been made
Fitzroy: Love every scar
Sole: Makes who we are
Lundy: Story so rare
Fishnet: Just us were there
Irish Sea: None ever knew
Shannon: What we went through
Rockall: If they were told
Malin: How strong and bold
Hebrides: Inspire to hear
Bailey: Despite such fear
Fair Isle: I hear the rain
Hebrides: Refreshed again
Southeast Iceland: Refreshed again

I Am The Dark The Light The Shade

I am the dark the light the shade
I'm every choice and not I've made
I'm each wrong path and questioned turn
Each revelation lesson learned

I am the sorrow and the glad
Each inspired thought and dream I've had
All my 'good nights' and weary sighs
I'm those regrets and pained goodbyes

I'm every joy and every fear
With every step that's brought me here
Had all those things not come to be
I would not stand just here as me

System Immiseration

Officials are reporting on system immiseration
A policy of poverty imposed upon our nation
Updated sanitised but chillingly reminds
The culture of the workhouse from past Victorian times

Ideological decisions continue to take down
The safety nets relied upon in villages and towns
The ministers state focus is firmly on employment
But even our key workers expect this cruel enjoyment

Deliberate choice in policy is cold and brutalising
Dependency on food banks for many normalising
The right to food restricted to what we call the wealthy
And families without denied their rights just to be healthy

Professor Alston laments on tragic disinvestment
Professor Deaton laments on pay remaining stagnant
Petitions and reports take their brief place in the news
But ministers maintain their stance and stubbornly refuse

Choices

The land we use to grow cheap meat
And other crops like corn and wheat
Sees other wildlife in retreat
This then our choices when we eat

Nitrogen fertilizers leak in water
Slurry from stock bound for the slaughter
Make rivers turn from clear to black
Their plants and creatures won't come back

Emissions heat our atmosphere
Destroys a healthy biosphere
This Earth we know keeps us alive
When will our choices see it thrive?

Fearful Journalists

Onward disclosure without authorisation
Measures preventing individual association
Restrictions on visiting a sensitive location
Fearful journalists in a global nation

Is it in the public interest such information?
What defence would be acceptable following this allegation?
Who would find themselves in jail on an article's publication?
Fearful journalists in a global nation

Reporters handed leaked documents expect incarceration
Their offices and homes could face investigation
For sharing with their readers a shocking revelation
Fearful journalists in a global nation

How reassuring the proposals are just out for consultation

Along the River Families Meet

Along the river families meet
To see the volunteers complete
Below St Thomas' hospital
A fitting live memorial

Beneath the plane trees leafy shade
The Posca red pen hearts won't fade
In dark the politicians walk
Denying relatives their talk

The clerics in communion
See what this movement has begun
Each heart a loved one gone too soon
Impacting every faith and none

This wall at least a one third mile
Each one of us can stop a while
And ask across to Parliament
Request it be made permanent

The Band of Ninety Two

I cast my vote a citizen
Knowing this right hard won
The lawmakers which govern me
Chosen by everyone
How comforting to know that
Though we may disagree
My people choose its leaders
A true democracy

Except

There is a band of ninety two
Who hold enormous sway
Sitting within the upper house
Some working day to day
As ministers who feel at ease
To judge or make the rules
Uninterested in common men
Uneducated fools

The barons lords and viscounts
Often the pale stale men
Hereditary peers who can
Sit in the Lords again
A tiny group can vote for these
Although it's just a few
Is this the reason power eludes
The likes of me and you?

NEDs

Oh to be a NED right now
And a pass to parliament
To walk the corridors of power
With serious intent

Old friends would pull the strings for me
To walk and wander free
With just a few days guaranteed
For a handsome salary

Not to provide much oversight
Although that is expected
Instead to keep my pals in power
Because we're all connected

But events have shed some light on me
My role is now debated
There's worry that so many get
Our jobs unregulated

While I am paid I have no wish
Or intent to scrutinize
Though I often hear the howling of
Democracy's pained cries

The Ministerial Code

Concerns are being raised
On what the public should be owed
By ministers who sign up to
The ministerial code

Appearing to be worthless
As rules but with no teeth
While expectations to comply
Apply to those beneath

Not one can be dismissed if they
So evidently break
Though others are admonished for
Less serious mistakes

Advisers with integrity
Are forced then to resign
So weary of a feeble code
And whispering malign

And all the while the trust
In institutions must erode
While ministers break wilfully
The ministerial code

Get Out the Horns and Tambourines

Ge out the horns and tambourines
Take penny whistles to the streets
Relearn the trumpet notes again
And fill the air with drumming beats

Fill up our lungs to shout and sing
Let cornets lead a dancing crowd
Swing giant rattles from our arms
And turn the music up too loud

Bang steel drums and cymbals too
Bring all the instruments to play
Until they hear they have no right
To take our protest rights away

Internal Family Systems

Manager says that everything's fine
Maintaining the peace to keep things in line
Paddling like crazy just staying afloat
Appearing so swan-like hates rocking the boat

Firefighter's distraction is fun for a while
But no one's convinced it's a happy lifestyle
Some common addiction might turn to more grief
For the hit just provides mere seconds relief

Exile sits hidden in a corner somewhere
Believing, mistaken, that nobody cares
Occasionally crying or screaming their pain
Till a sibling instructs to be quiet again

Self is the parent or leader of three
Respecting each one has rights just to be
Hearing their stories but calm patiently
In loving each part sets the whole person free

An Expert in Our Language

An expert in our language
Of political communication
Has just handed in a survey
On the thinking of our nation

There's concern that capitalism's
Not respected as it should be
So the wording might be changing
Talking more of markets and free

Word like workers don't enthuse us
Employees is more appealing
As for those high earning bosses
Most think CEOs are stealing

Whether through some rate avoidance
Or receiving public handouts
Corporation tax abuses
May think it's so without doubt

But the other side sees different
With too many getting money
Means the hardest working voters
Have to pay and that's not funny

So the think tanks will start working
Recommending words we'll favour
Finding phrases in our language
To ensure they keep our labour

If business doesn't stir us
Other nouns will try persuading
For the language of its leaders
Has to keep the free world trading

All Things to All People

I am all things to all people
Canvas blank for your projection
Of your preference I'll support it
To protect me from rejection

I will say what my advisers
Tell me what you'll want to hear
Wear a hard hat in a lorry
While I hold a pint of beer

Deny anything I've written
With which you might disagree
While my jolly nice persona
Will convince you to like me

Hope your nature will require you
To hear what you want to hear
While some messages get through and
All the others disappear

Laying Tracks for Rails

As drills for excavation
Bore into our sloping hills
Alarm is being raised
About its exponential bills

A whisper is transforming
Into a mighty roar
As more are left to wonder
At what this track is for

Whilst residents find floodlights
Create disruptive sleep
And roads are blocked to access
The invoices pile deep

Now ministers are once again
Accused of breaking code
To get the bill through Royal Assent
Down played the money owed

Never it seems will such a line
Advantage such a few
Since now we've learned how online calls
Across the miles will do

So too our ancient woodland
Sees long lived arbors fall
And those who don't make journeys
Won't benefit at all

Meanwhile in other news
Our foreign aid loses a slice
Because we can't afford to help the poor
And that's not nice

How can we be expected
To pay out while in debt
While laying tracks for rails
It's almost certain we'll regret?

We Interrupt This Broadcast

We interrupt this broadcast
To make you look away
While we get on with doing
What's our business of the day

Such fierce debates can fill
The morning phone in radio shows
Discussing one incendiary line
We hear your anger grow

Whilst bills removing rights
Pass peacefully towards assent
And creeping corporate takeover
Ensures support is lent

These petty small controversies
Or sometimes culture wars
Divide district effectively
What else can they be for?

Debating the Merits of Capitalism

I cannot trust my children's school
To fully educate
With capitalism's theory now
Removed from the debate

No noisy group discussions
On its merits will be heard
Among the desks and corridors
To me this seems absurd

Are many of those hard exams
My child will need to pass
Preparing them to merely serve
The capitalist class?

To not allow a child to question
What a job is for
Or who will benefit from
Keeping working people poor?

Do free markets hurt nature?
That should deserve some learning
Is that why people have no food?
Or why forests keep burning?

At least allow a child to know
Which system dominates
And then decide its merits
And how it educates

Ministerial Portfolio

Should there be a new portfolio
A ministerial post
A Minister for Planet Earth
Is what's required most

The Chancellor would move along
When they joined the Cabinet
Their brief to change the world for good
The most ambitious yet

They'd state that they would focus on
Our nature and its health
This would be deemed to surely be
The nation's greatest wealth

The quality of air we breathe
Would now be quantified
Its metrics superceding those
The Treasury provide

A key task would be counting flowers
And bees which they support
This would be much more pressing then
The goods that we export

And cleaning up our waters
They'd make it very clear
Would have much greater prominence
Than GDP that year

More than household consumption
Which can't go on and on
They'd speak up for the very Earth
Each Minister lives on

Welcomed Here

From Syrian border to Manchester
This child of ours find refuge there
With each step puppeteers retrace
The journey of our human race

Crowds gather as they wish to see
This walk of shared humanity
From Jungle first within a play
The set a domed Afghan cafe

She left only so we could see
The life of all child refugees
Those children who still disappear
Alone afraid consumed by fear

Each stranger wants to be her friend
To welcome home at journey's end
This nine year old child is welcomed here
Such is the power of theatre

Contract Terminated

No friendly chat
That's so outdated
An email 'Contract
Terminated'
Nothing personal
It's business see
No respect for
My humanity
The algorithm
Knew my route
Dispensing with
Futile dispute
I'd signed up on
Their app it's true
Did not require
An interview
They did not know
Me just for me
Why know my
Personality?
A short term role
For extra pay
To supplement
The day to day
So feeling sad
Deleted my
Usual app
From which I buy
Such habits can be
Hard to break
But worth it for my
Conscience sake

Just a Story

Was it fiction or fact?
We weren't showered in glory
Narratives can detract
But it's still just a story

Where did the lines blur
When we mixed in some doubt?
And why should we still care
If there's details left out?

If it's in black and white
Can there still be dispute?
Each side says they were right
That's the truth absolute

Human beings as we are
And our need to be right
We can stop seeing clear
Sets us up for a fight

We can see differently
So let's see conflict cease
For we both can agree
Now's the time to make peace

Lunchtime at the Bank

Engels walked here in horror to see
The squalid streets and poverty
The famine fleers poorly fed
Into this depot for the dead

Housed near the cotton city's mills
No comfort from its winter chills
He saw the workers graves en masse
Conditions of the working class

And now I stand on the fifteenth floor
Above the ghosts who left the poor
See lunchtime workers at their rest
Among the greens kept at their best

Collecting debts approving loans
Descendents still requiring homes
A hope ancestors never had
Aspiring to a city pad

New Democracy

Where Henry Hunt took to the stage
The crowd ensured the hussars rage
Poor families gathered peacefully
To listen to his oratory

From northern towns without MPs
Deserving of democracy
These workers tired of labour dumped
Left penniless when trading slumped

The media barons of the day
Revised the story to their way
Blamed people for the violence met
But onlookers could not forget

The regent lending his support
Pleased of the way the soldiers fought
The magistrates who'd earned his praise
Arranged trials for the coming days

Now children by this very hall
Seek climate care and hope for all
This place of protest still will see
A hopeful new democracy

The British Worker

The British worker is among
The most lazy on Earth
No concept of hard graft they learn
Bad habits right from birth

They work the fewest hours
And need too many breaks
Sometimes they might get ill
And need time off for Goodness sake

As Ministers in waiting
We look on them with despair
But hope our future policies
Will make them be aware

Our citizens are valued
By the cash they generate
And we'll show them what hard work is
When we're Ministers of State

Gender Pain Gap

I'm sorry but I don't have time
To understand your pain
Best to go home relax a bit
And don't come back again

A few days off might be the best
Try not to ruminate
I've seen women like you before
They can exaggerate

The history of your pain will take
Too long for me to hear
We only have ten minutes and
I haven't got all year

It's not a subject that we tend
To research for your kind
Females can be so difficult
It's probably your mind

One hopes that in a hundred years
We'll be much more aware
No challenge to be managed just
A human needing care

New Opium

The sigh of an oppressed creature
The heart of a heartless state
The soul of soulless conditions
Becomes an opiate

Shrines built in shiny kitchens
Our priests preach on the screen
This congregation still exchanges
Power for dopamine

A Transformation

A word spoken
An explosion felt
A knot in stomach
A journey planned
A conflict anticipated
A chair emptied
A decision feared
A shame swallowed
An invitation received
An opportunity to join
A conversation listened to
An outcome told
An opinion given
A chance to respond
A question asked
A lie chosen
A crowd spoken to
A circle outside of
A room to belong
A freezing melted
A kiss wanted
A brushed cheek
An intimate encounter
A threat hanging
An opportunity missed
A letter arriving
A response required

A Transformation cont.

An anniversary remembered
A card chosen
A goodbye regretted
A bereavement felt
A sigh piercing
A scream suppressed
A failure crushing
A reminder unwelcomed
A hospital appointment
A results confirmation
A photograph found
A mother loved
A glass filled again
A child's birth
A baby held
A gathering of butterflies
A newsflash
A combustible material
A door slammed
A spark ignited
A guest visiting
A room to prepare
An unexpected meeting
A trap set
A secret exposed
A smashed plate
A found key
A window unlocked